IMAGES
of America

LYNDON

Dedicated to my children, Lois, Kermit, and Janet,
and to my grandchildren and great-grandchildren,
to share with them the heritage
of my home town.

NESTLED IN A LITTLE VALLEY. This peaceful scene, *c.* 1890, looks northeast from Harris Hill over the village of Lyndonville. The surrounding hills give it the appearance of a village in a bowl. Burke Mountain, center, about 10 miles away, can be seen from many places in the town of Lyndon.

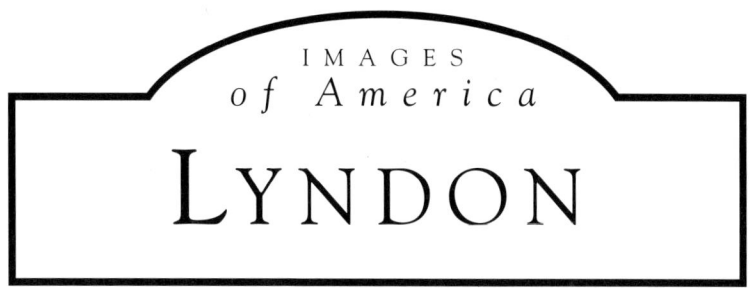

IMAGES
of America

LYNDON

Harriet Fletcher Fisher

Under the auspices of the Lyndon Historical Society

ARCADIA

First published 1998
Copyright © Harriet Fletcher Fisher, 1998

ISBN 0-7524-0915-8

Published by Arcadia Publishing,
an imprint of the Chalford Publishing Corporation,
One Washington Center, Dover, New Hampshire 03820.
Printed in Great Britain

Library of Congress Cataloging-in-Publication Data applied for

ROLLING HILLS NORTHWARD. This image depicts Lyndon Center, c. 1900. The Lyndon
Institute building, Thompson Hall, is to the left, and the Baptist church is in the center of the
image. The town-owned cemetery is seen at the center of the photograph. Though the hills
have grown to forest again, there are many clearings with dozens and dozens of houses.

Contents

Acknowledgments

The publication of this book is possible because of the help of many generous people who willingly shared and entrusted me with their cherished photographs to supplement my own extensive collection. Thank you, Edwin and Beryle Houghton, Patricia Riley Leslie, Mary Spencer, Lucinda Hunter, Merlyn Courser, Esther Merriam Gray, Jack and Richard Cheney, Alan and Denise Parent, Philip Mathewson, Allan Bean, Loretta McClure, Kay Switser, Deanna Wheeler, John King, Eric Chester, Charles Lang, Kermit Fisher (Fisher Field and Fenton Chester Arena photographs), and *That Book Store*. Thanks also to Rosemary Secord of *Green Mountain Books and Prints*, who encouraged me to use photographs from the postcard collection of the late Ralph Secord at the Cobleigh Public Library; to Lucinda Hill at Vermont Tap & Die; Rhonda Paris at the Dairy Association Company; Tonya West at the *Lyndon Independent*; Michael Wheeler at the Lyndon Outing Club; Kathie Heroux at the Lyndon Institute Alumni office; Lyndon State College (the Vail Museum collection); Lyndon Town Historian and Shores Memorial Museum curator, Ruth Hopkins McCarty, for her time in helping me select Lyndon Historical Society photographs, many of them from Kenneth Barber's Peterson Collection, and from the archives for the Lyndon town history. Last, but by no means least, special thanks go to A. Richard Boera for the countless hours he spent with the layout and editing of the book to help make it ready for publication.

Introduction

Lyndon, Vermont, in Caledonia County is comprised of Lyndon Corner, where the town originated; Lyndon Center, the second part of early settlements; Lyndonville, an incorporated village within the town; and the outer town area that was once almost all family farms. There are the usual place names, generally former school districts, such as Mt. Hunger, Pudding Hill, Little Egypt, Diamond Hill, Mosquito District, Squabble Hollow, Red Village, Happytown, Hell Hollow, Swaggerham, and others. Lyndon was chartered November 20, 1780; the record in the town clerk's office bears the date June 27, 1781, after its survey. The town of 24,256 acres has a river running through it—the Passumpsic (Abnaki for "clear waters")—that has many crossings. Fortunately, five covered bridges remain, the most sought-after tourist attractions in the area.

The origin of the town's name is not clear, but it seems most likely that it was chosen to honor Josias Lyndon, a distinguished political associate of most of the original petitioners for the land grant and ex-governor of their home state of Rhode Island. An alternate version has it named for Josias Lyndon Arnold, eldest son of the leader of the new township, proprietor Jonathan Arnold. Providence resident Josias Lyndon, Arnold's good friend, had been elected governor (of Rhode Island) just a few days before the child's birth. Both versions could be accurate, the name equally honoring both friend and first son.

Lyndon Corner and Lyndon Center gave up incorporated village status in 1962 and are now under the general town government. The village of Lyndonville, governed by a board of trustees, was born in 1866 with the building of the Connecticut and Passumpsic Rivers Railroad shops on farmland north of the Corner and east of the Center. Toward the end of the nineteenth century, Lyndonville had grown so rapidly that it began replacing Lyndon (Corner) as "the center of things," and the Corner became a place of residence.

Boston papers dubbed Lyndon a tough town because of bootlegging activities during Prohibition. Being hardy Lyndonites, we turned this into a compliment for ourselves, developing the nickname of "A Town Too Tough To Die." We survived disastrous fires in 1894 and 1924, the railroad strike of 1922, the destructive flood of 1927, and a hurricane in 1938, as well as the Great Depression. A few Lyndon citizens turned to bootlegging, partly for the money, no doubt, and possibly for the adventure and excitement in those days of hard times.

There was always something good going on, too, as evidenced in many stories published in the *Lyndonville Journal*. On July 1, 1896—during an era when bicycling was very popular—the newspaper suggested, "You should drop into Lyndonville some fine June evening and see the whole population awheel, singly, in pairs, groups, platoons, and brigades." Said the editor, "I am credibly informed that there are 26 different secret societies in town and 18 good halls." There were other clubs and organizations as well. The Village Improvement Society was only one of the active groups that generated plenty of things for people to do. There were skating parties, either on the frozen Passumpsic or on a village rink, sliding parties, dances, drama, musicals, and many other functions that kept everybody happy at a time when people found their entertainment in their home or in town. Church-sponsored activities were prevalent as well. Besides, there were many special train excursions where people could easily attend some major function taking place in other towns north or south of Lyndonville.

There are bound to be some subjects omitted from this book. There was no intention of ignoring important aspects of life in Lyndon. The Morgan horse, for example, was of great importance here. Many of the horses in the winter races were Morgans in the days when the horses worked during the week and raced on Saturdays. In some cases, no photographs were available, and in others, they were too faded to reproduce. Much of our photography is dated by the changes after the fires, or by the appearance of electric light poles, automobiles, or additions of new buildings. People just weren't in the habit of dating their photographs.

It is fortunate that we have so many old photographs available—besides generous individual contributions—due in great measure, to the untiring efforts of the late Dr. Venila Lovina Shores. In the 1960s and 70s, she made appointments with Jenks Studio in St. Johnsbury and took borrowed photographs to the studio for immediate copying. She then returned the photographs to the owners and kept the negatives in the town vault for future use in the town history. Many had not been used, and, after all these years, many were returned to the Jenks Studio, which did a fine job of making prints for this publication.

The late Paul Aubin—jeweler, musician, designer of our Christmas Crown of Lights as well as the symbol for the Snowflake Festival and the Veterans Memorial—used to talk about the many special things about Lyndon: the volunteer fire department and rescue squad, the Outing Club, the ice arena, the Powers Park pool, the band, the parades, scouting, youth sports, the Cobleigh Library, Lyndon Institute and Lyndon State College, the beautiful parks, the hills and valleys, and above all the four seasons. Many of us here in town agree—"Right on, Paul!"

One
Scenic Lyndon

SCENIC AND SIGNIFICANT. Lyndon's first town meeting was held in Daniel Reniff's log cabin on a Lyndon hillside. The marker, made and set by Luther B. Harris, is near the site where the log cabin stood. Now called Vail Hill Road, this spot looks down over the road to Wheelock. The meeting was warned by town officers of Wheelock, which had already been established.

THE SCHOOLHOUSE BRIDGE AT LYNDON CORNER. This *c.* 1925 photograph became known far-and-wide when Elisabeth Chase used it on boxes of the maple candy fancy assortment made at her home near the bridge. When it became inadequate for modern traffic, the Town built a by-pass road to save this bit of Lyndon heritage.

ONE OF FIVE COVERED BRIDGES IN LYNDON. The Sanborn Bridge settled in a new location on the Passumpsic River beside the Lynburke Motel. Formerly the crossing between Lyndonville and Lyndon Center, it was moved across town in 1960 to make way for a concrete bridge. Herbert Gallagher and Armand Morin "pooled their resources" and bought the bridge for $1 in order to save this highly regarded example of Paddleford construction.

FOLSOM'S CROSSING BRIDGE. The photograph was taken January 29, 1916. Alfred Smith, who lived nearby, watched this covered bridge topple over into the Passumpsic River, just north of Lyndonville, in the November 1927 flood.

A WELL-BUILT CONCRETE BRIDGE. This bridge can please the eye, though probably not as much as the picturesque covered bridge it replaced here at Folsom's Crossing. The concrete span was built immediately after the great flood of 1927 by Frank Calkins of Danville.

11

LYNDONVILLE AND BURKE MOUNTAIN. Pictured here on March 18, 1916, the mountain is now a developed ski area.

AN EARLY SNOWSTORM. On November 14, 1916, Railroad Park and Williams Street were covered with enough snow for this horse and sled to be out rounding the corner by the lamp post from Broad Street into Depot Street. The baggage cart on the railroad platform (left), a loading platform, and the watering trough (right) are covered with snow. The engine at the far right may be clearing the track, and the St. Elizabeth Church overlooks all.

JACK FROST'S LATEST. Though unusually late for ice, May 10, 1900, it makes a pretty picture on Railroad Park. The passenger station is on the right. The block on the left was newly built by George Ide after the great fire of 1894. The store on the left is Parker's and the right window reads, "Campbell & Blodgett, Insurance." The bicycle is probably the one E.M. Campbell rode back and forth between his home in Lyndon Center and his business in Lyndonville.

DEPOT STREET ON A RAINY NIGHT. Not many people ventured out, it appears, but the street glistens under the electric lights, *c.* 1950.

A Cool Splash in the Fountain. In Lyndonville's beautiful park *c.* 1930, people could sit on the benches and watch the children play or rest after shopping in the nearby stores. Enjoying the splashing fountain and cool green grass, shaded by elm and maple trees, could be a welcome respite on a hot summer day.

Lyndon Terraces. A.G. Pratt built this terraced hill in Lyndon Corner because his wife didn't like the "flat view" seen from the window of their house across the road. The hill was built mostly from clay drawn in by horses and terraced so that Mrs. Pratt would have something beautiful to look at. The terraced hill disappeared when an off-ramp from Interstate 91 was built here.

SCENIC BACK ROADS. These secluded roads were favorite places for Sunday drives. This image was taken on Hog Street near a busy working farm in the autumn of 1937. It is now a much-traveled paved thoroughfare known as Lily Pond Road. With housing developments and the Lyndon Town School on this road, school buses and many cars buzz along here morning and afternoon, and not just a few in-between.

A PLEASANT DRIVE IN THE COUNTRY? Not during mud season on dirt roads. "This is as far as I go," the driver must have thought and then got out to take this picture, May 4, 1918.

A Brook, a Bridge, and a Border of Trees. These landmarks comprised a pretty scene at Lyndon Corner. The G.C. and G.W. Cahoon houses are seen behind the trees. A Cahoon ancestor was the first settler in the town of Lyndon.

Moonlight at Railroad Grove. All is quiet on this moonlit winter night in Camp Grove, just off the center of Main Street, Lyndonville. The buildings were taken down when it became Powers Park, a community playground, in 1915.

Two
The Country

A COUNTRY HOME. This old log house built in 1818 was really plank. Also known as Old Grandma Pierce House, it stood on a spot in the 335 acres of farmland that in 1866–67 became the village of Lyndonville. The house was condemned and burned down in 1893 because someone had died of typhoid fever there. Luckily, W.H. Fletcher took this photograph in 1885.

THREE FARMS. All three farms can be seen in this *c.* 1930 photograph. Gullies, erosion exposing sand, a brook, hills, and valleys were natural hazards for the nine-hole golf course on the farm, in center foreground, that was run by the Lyndon Golf Club from the late 1800s until around 1955. It was also the farm's pasture for the Holstein cattle herd.

THE ABNAKI GOLF CLUBHOUSE. During its heyday, this club was a hub of activity. When the Lyndon Golf Club was reactivated after World War I, the clubhouse was torn down because it had deteriorated from disuse.

CULTIVATING CORN IN HADLEYVILLE WITH A LOT OF HELP. This was one way to spend the Fourth of July in 1917.

HIGH DRIVE. The name of this type of ramp—high drive—was common to several Lyndon farms. In many cases the stables were in the lower part and the hay stored overhead, affording an easy way for the hay to be pitched down to the stable and put into the cows' mangers. This *c.* 1920 barn was on the Blake Farm on Pudding Hill.

EVERYBODY HELPED WITH THE HAYING. This *c.* 1905 photograph depicts Farmer Fletcher and his daughter pitching on the hay. His son-in-law on the wagon spreads the hay so it won't roll off when the horses draw it to the barn. In the meantime, the son rakes up the scattering with the dump rake.

GREAT-GRANDMA DOES THE SPINNING. Wool and flax raised on the farm was spun, woven, and made into clothing. The finely woven flax was also made into bed linens. (People weren't so apt to go to the dentist in those days but got along without teeth, especially when older, and probably had good strong gums!)

THE SHEEP ARE IN THE MEADOW, THE CHICKS ARE EATING CORN. These images would be typical farm scenes in the late 1800s and early 1900s—especially before the Lyndonville Creamery was established and many farmers went into dairying. It was generally the custom for a farmer's wife to take care of the hens and keep the egg money for her own use.

THE ROAD TO VAIL'S. A buggy takes the scenic road to Theodore N. Vail's Speedwell Farms on the hill. A visitor to Speedwell Farms describes the road from Lyndon Center in the October 23, 1911 *Boston Transcript,* "The remainder of the way was uphill, over a macadam road as smooth as a billiard table and lined with young shade trees." This was the first paved road in the state of Vermont, built by Vail for the convenience of himself and his visitors.

THE SNOWROLLER AT SPEEDWELL FARMS. In this 1920 photograph, Ernest Allard is driving the double team to roll T.N. Vail's farm and home properties. Some rollers that worked the public roads were larger. The drivers dressed in fur coats and covered their knees with buffalo robes. At noontime, they would drive into a farmer's yard, put blankets and feedbags on the horses, and come into the kitchen to get warm and eat their lunch.

MANSION-IN-THE-MAKING. Between 1903 and 1908, Elmer Darling, a Burke native who had made a fortune in New York's Fifth Avenue Hotel, built a mansion for his retirement. Mr. Darling may be one of the men on the porch roof with his horse and buggy parked at the side. He was no doubt checking up on the progress of his new residence.

THE MANSION FINISHED. The structure at the end of the portico is the billiard room. Darling named his residence Burklyn Hall because the house straddled the Burke-Lyndon town line. He raised Morgan horses and Registered Jersey cows on his extensive country estate. He was a generous benefactor of both towns.

A SPRING OUTING. The wooden paddles some group members are holding would indicate that this group of happy people have just enjoyed sugar-on-snow at a sugarhouse in the woods where there still would have been some snow even on April 22, 1917.

Three

The Railroad Gives Birth to a Village

THE RAILROAD ROUNDHOUSE. A story is told that the fireman and the engineer were trying to get their engine into the roundhouse, but it kept going in and out until one of them finally hollered, "If we get it in again, shut the door!"

THE BOSTON & MAINE RAILROAD. The Connecticut & Passumpsic Rivers Railroad and shops were leased by the Boston & Maine Railroad (B & M) in 1887. In 1926, the Canadian Pacific Railway leased the road and shops from B & M and acquired ownership in 1946. The line between Wells River and Newport was designated the Lyndonville subdivision. The railroad shops were built by the Connecticut & Passumpsic Rivers Railroad after the shops in St. Johnsbury burned down on March 21, 1866. The company rebuilt and expanded their operations on 335 acres of farmland acquired from Benjamin Sanborn in Lyndon. The first brick was laid August 1, 1866. Every week, the *Vermont Union*, the newspaper published at the Corner, reported the progress of the exciting operations going on at the "new village," 2.5 miles north. The village grew rapidly. George Walker built a large hotel on what was being called Depot Street and applied for a post office. He received his appointment as "postmaster of Lyndonville" on April 13, 1868, and the new village got its name.

RAILROAD SHOP. This photograph depicts one of the shops when it was the Boston & Maine. Beginning with the Connecticut & Passumpsic Rivers Railroad, this thriving business employed a lot of men for many years and, eventually, even some women at offices in the Depot. At first the company could not make out a check to a woman. An early female dispatcher's pay was included as time-and-a-half for her husband in his paycheck! When railroad workers went on strike nationwide on July 1, 1922, three hundred Lyndonville shopmen, who had plenty of repair work ahead, obeyed the strike order and walked off their jobs with only six or seven remaining on the job. As a result of the strike, some workers sought jobs elsewhere and moved away.

"Coffee Break" for a Photograph. One worker watches from an upper window, *c.* 1890. The Connecticut & Passumpsic Rivers Railroad erected sturdy and handsome brick buildings. Many are gone today, taken down brick by brick.

Section Gangs. This one had a 10-mile stretch to cover, keeping tracks cleared and repaired. Two men pumped the handles up and down to propel the handcar along the track. A good pumping took the men to the appointed section. This unidentified crew is stopped by the Lyndon (Corner) station, probably in the early 1900s.

A Railroad Company House and Family. This photograph was taken in the 1880s. The railroad company built many houses similar to this in the new village (that became Lyndonville) it created when the company built the shops and all the necessary buildings for conducting the railroad business here. These company houses were sturdily built; this one has been remodeled and is occupied by descendants of a railroad family.

Aaron Twombly's Four-Tenement House. Built in 1882 on Broad Street, this house had fancy trimmings and a brick foundation. The Music Hall, built in 1884, can be seen at the left. Twombly's house and his store on the next lot, corner of Broad and Depot Streets, burned in the 1894 conflagration.

THE FIRST DEPOT STREET. Twombly's store is seen facing Broad Street in this photograph. The large building (far right) was Walker's Hotel, the site of the first post office in the new Lyndonville. The hotel burned down in 1869. The railroad station is the brick building in the foreground.

AN OLD BOSTON & MAINE WOODBURNER. It was scrapped in 1899, but the photograph was taken before 1894, when all of Depot Street, seen behind the engine, was burned. The Mathewson Block in the background, actually on Main Street, did not burn.

MANSION ON THE PARK. Hubbard Hastings, cashier of the Connecticut & Passumpsic Rivers Railroad, built this elegant home in 1867 on Park Street. It was the first mansion in the new village of Lyndonville. It was said to have the finest cellar and barn in town. The Pettigrew family occupied the home for 30 years.

CASTLE ON THE PARK. Julia Pettigrew Hutchins inherited the house and remodeled it in 1896 into an even more elegant home, designed by Lambert Packard. The *Vermont Union* described it as "an architectural ornament of the village." The icehouse (at right) was turned into a cool retreat for summer tea parties. The house still stands in its rebuilt splendor facing the beautiful village park. This photograph was taken in October 1983, then the Boera family home.

THE SECOND DEPOT STREET. The street was rebuilt after the big fire of 1894. The Masonic Block raised a flag on a tall flagpole. On the left, facing Broad Street, is the new Lyndonville Bank. Almost all of the 36 burned-out stores and offices went back into business in fine new blocks. Salmon Stern, who had bought the Twombly building on the corner, replaced it with the three-story block. On the right is George Ide's replacement block.

SHOPPING DAY IN LYNDONVILLE. This all burned in 1894. The location is on the north side of Depot Street about halfway between Church and Main Streets. In the center building are Eastman and Co., grocer; Mrs. Young, ladies' furnishings; and W.D. Poole, boots and shoes. There were tenements upstairs, and on the right is a barbershop—a magnifying glass will show barber poles in front.

A BUSY STREET. Though there are lots of cars, the hitching posts are still in place. The Corner Boarding House is at left. On the right is the Cobleigh Public Library built in 1906 as benefactor Eber W. Cobleigh requested. Another familiar sight in Lyndonville was the "silent policeman," one at each intersection on Depot Street, each with a sign that read, "Keep to the Right," like the one in the foreground.

THE THIRD DEPOT STREET. After the upper half of Depot Street (both sides) burned in January 1924, the Realty Block (on right) replaced the Ide and Masonic Blocks. Good-old faithful Mathewson Block (facing) was not affected by this fire, and it barely escaped the one in 1894. The structure survived a localized fire in 1996 and was restored after being badly gutted.

33

THE NICHOLS BLOCK. Located on the north side of Depot Street, Nichols Block is pictured here *c.* 1893. Salmon Stern is standing on the ramp in front of his dry goods store. J.C. Eaton appears in the doorway of his hardware store, and the insurance office upstairs is probably that of Campbell & Blodgett.

STREET LAMPS. When he was a young lad, W.E. Riley used to light this lamp that stood by Twombly's store. When these lamps were no longer used, he acquired this one for a keepsake. In recent years, his daughter, Patricia Riley Leslie, donated it to the Lyndon Historical Society. During Lyndon's Bicentennial in 1991, Eric Chester set it up as shown here, and lit the kerosene wick to show how it worked.

Four
Around the Town

HIGH WATER IN HADLEYVILLE. Looking toward Lyndon Center, the Baptist church steeple is seen a little right of center. It is quite normal for the Passumpsic River to slip over its banks somewhat in the spring, but on April 22, 1917, the area appears to be experiencing a bit more than the usual springtime overflow.

AN 1895 MAKEOVER. John G. Hadley (left) sold his steam mill to Ulysses Grant (second from left) on January 18, 1895, who made it over into a paint shop. Hadley retained the carpenter shop on the right. For many years and several generations, "Lys" Grant painters included sons, cousins, nephews, and brothers. Ulysses Sheridan Grant was born in 1864, in Concord, Vermont. For many years he and other Grants were drummers in the Grant-Nichols Drum Corps based in Concord. Lys also played the bass drum in the Lyndonville Military Band. After Grant died in 1945, Maurice Nurenberg bought the paint shop and used it for storing used goods he bought and sold. Around 1963, Sidney Nurenberg tore down the old building and built an office there for his real estate business. The office was eventually converted into a modest house.

LYNDON BEGAN IN LYNDON CORNER. The Dana Block (left) still stands today as do some of the other buildings. The street is the present Route 5, south of Lyndonville. A public telephone is available in the block, according to the sign on the post. This photograph was taken *c.* 1900.

TODAY'S ROUTE 5 BEFORE PAVING. This *c.* 1915 photograph shows Lys Grant's paint shop on right in the center of the section known as Hadleyville. Today the residence on the left is gone and there is a strip with businesses and stores along Memorial Drive (Route 5) between Lyndon Corner and Lyndonville.

LYNDON CENTER POST OFFICE AND STORE. When you picked up your mail, you could also get your canned tomatoes, Quaker Oats, and other groceries. At left is Perley Davis and to the right is George Rines, who was postmaster at the Center from 1912 to 1919. The Lyndon Center post office was commissioned in 1829, only two years after the first post office in Lyndon (Corner) was established.

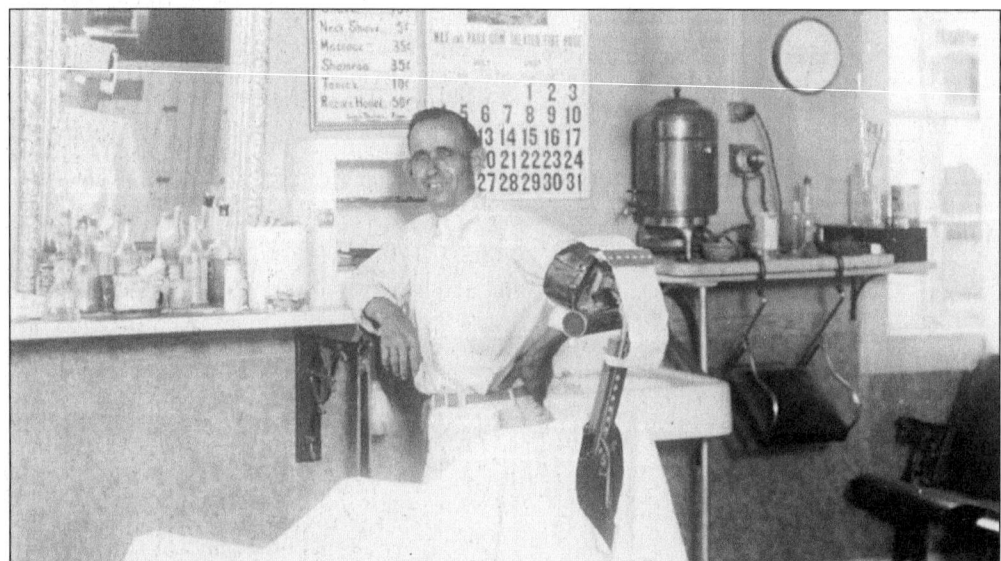

SHORT OF STATURE, TALL WHEN SALUTING THE AMERICAN FLAG. When Louis Thomas was about 12 years old, his parents sent him to America after one son was shot down in the Greek and Ottoman Empire war. "Louie" served in World War I. He opened a barber shop in Lyndon Corner around 1928. He was an expert on flag etiquette, active in the American Legion and the fire department, and loved to dance. The calendar says 1937.

EARTH MOVERS. This was the way a bridge was built, *c.* 1914. When T.N. Vail built the pond and bridge by Lyndon Institute, it was with horsepower and manpower.

A SHORT CUT. This swing bridge was a short-cut from Lyndon Center to Lyndonville. Men living in Lyndon Center could swing over the Passumpsic River to the railroad shops in Lyndonville. Horace Locklin (left) and Charles Parker are the men on the bridge, *c.* 1904.

Town and Meetinghouse. This is the oldest public building still standing in town. In 1800, some townspeople organized the Religious Society for the Purpose of Promoting Public Preaching of the Gospel. This society wanted land at the center of town for the meetinghouse, a burying ground, and a common or parade ground where the militia could practice. In 1801, Job Sheldon deeded 6 acres to the town for the house, which was finally erected in 1809. The Town of Lyndon contributed toward the building cost for the privilege of using it for public meetings. It was originally two stories high with 54 box pews and a balcony above. Around 1859, the belfry was removed and the roof lowered, making the building one story. The high box pulpit and the pews were removed. Since 1971, town meetings have been held at Lyndon Institute. The Town House is still used for public functions and meetings. The building at the right is the old Lyndon Center School, which, after 1900, was used to store cemetery equipment.

MR. VERMONT. W. Arthur Simpson (1887–1971), a Lyndon native, family man, and owner of a Milking Shorthorn dairy farm in East Lyndon, was known for his wisdom and humor. He was a longtime public servant—a school director, selectman, town representative, state senator, member of the State Highway Board, Old Age Assistance Commissioner, and Social Welfare Commissioner. He retired in 1959, but the pull was strong and he became Lyndon town representative in 1963 and 1965. He served his state for over 50 years under 13 governors. Governor Philip Hoff dubbed him "Mr. Vermont." Mr. Simpson quoted easily from the Bible and when asked about this ability his answer was, "Well, when I was a boy going to Sunday school in East Lyndon, I got a Bible for perfect attendance and I thought I was supposed to read it!"

TAVERN IN THE TOWN. The tavern stood from 1807 to 1897. The Lyndon House was an important hotel on the main route from Boston to Montreal. Lyndon Corner thrived with industries, an academy, two churches, several stores, a bank, post office, and a dance hall over the hotel carriage house; the hotel bar was legendary. The train came in the 1850s and the Lyndon station was only a mile away. There was the equivalent of taxi service by horse and buggy or sleigh to the hotel. After the hotel burned in 1897, travelers went on to Lyndonville. By then, because of the railroad operation, the village of Lyndonville had grown rapidly and with the loss of the hotel, people began to gravitate toward what was fast becoming the center of things. This photograph was taken in 1893.

Lyndon Center Baptist Church. The Free Baptists organized in 1802; they were the first denomination in town to do so. After their church (built in 1816) on Pudding Hill closed, they met elsewhere until this one was built at the Center in 1848. A man works on the steeple while his horse waits below.

Oldest Church in Town. The Congregational church was organized in 1817 at Lyndon Corner. Until the church was erected and dedicated in 1829, the congregation met at members' homes or in the schoolhouse. A yearly service and a few other uses, such as an occasional wedding, keeps the church in the hands of the congregation. This photograph was taken c. 1918.

LUTHER BURNHAM HARRIS (1847–1913).
The town benefactor poses here in his Grand Army of the Republic (GAR) uniform. He served in Company D, Vermont Volunteers during the Civil War. In Andersonville and other Confederate prisons, he kept a diary that is now in the University of Vermont archives. After the war he became a civil engineer, working on bridges for the Union Pacific Railroad pushing west. He returned to Vermont, lived in Lyndon Center, became a banker and a civic leader, and collected antiques, relics, foreign art, and a valuable library.

THE WILD BOAR FOUNTAIN AT LYNDON CENTER. The fountain was cast in Pietro Tacca's original mold in Florence, Italy, and placed in this little park by Luther B. Harris. This was only the second Wild Boar fountain in all America at the time—the other being in the Metropolitan Museum of Art in New York City. Theodore Roosevelt stopped here to admire the sculpture when his Bull Moose campaign car came by in 1912.

CENTENARIAN JOHN DUTTON (1802–1905).
Dutton, a retired farmer, had this photograph taken on his 101st birthday, September 2, 1903. He was the initiator of the subscription for the Revolutionary War memorial monument. The subscribers to the monument, an important feature in the Lyndon Center cemetery, were mostly descendants of the soldiers named on the memorial.

REVOLUTIONARY WAR SOLDIERS MEMORIAL. In 1858, more than one hundred Lyndon men cared enough to subscribe to a monument commemorating Revolutionary War soldiers who lived in Lyndon. Though Lyndon was not yet a town during that war and soldiers were not from Lyndon, a number lived in Lyndon later. Their names are all engraved on the monument, standing tall at the top of the slope in the oldest part of the cemetery.

THE SLEEPING BABE. "A dreamless sleep, emblem of eternal rest." Gratis P. Spencer (1825–1908), stonecutter, fashioned this beautiful monument. The sleeping child seems to represent his five children that died very young. A rosebud at the child's back is a symbol of a life unfolded. This monument is sought out by many curious people who have heard of the atheistic sayings carved on the rims of the monument. The story has been told that some church members tried to eradicate the inscriptions. They would probably be glad to know that through the years, because marble does wear down, most of the words are now very hard to read. His wife's name, Annette Caswell, appears on the other side.

Five

Around the Village

A Covered Bridge Sailing up Main Street. It may seem a bit odd but in 1960 the bridge was saved and moved north about a mile-and-a-half from its original location, spanning the Passumpsic River between Lyndonville and Lyndon Center, to make way for a modern concrete bridge. (See page 10.)

MASONIC BLDG, LYNDONVILLE VT.

THE MASONIC BUILDING (1895–1924). When the street burned in 1894, this elegant block, impressive enough to grace a city, rose on the corner of Depot and Church Streets. The date, 1895, in large raised numerals appears high above the third-story window. On the side, along the top, are the words in raised letters, "Masonic Building." The handsome storefronts enticed customers, and the jewelry store clock on the street really told the time, easily seen by passengers as the train came into the station, right of photograph. The second floor contained apartments, and the GAR Hall occupied the third floor. Edmunds-Druggists has the corner store, and beyond the hanging watch we find the Lapoint Bros. meat market. This great building was around less than 30 years, because it burned in the January 21, 1924 fire, as well as the Ide Block shown beside it.

JEWELRY OR INSURANCE? You could go to James Dexter's jewelry store in the Masonic Block and purchase a watch or have one repaired (note watches with tags on board at left); a clock appears to interest the lady. Or you could cross the aisle and buy insurance or order coal from Campbell & Blodgett, just on the other side of the store. They sold bicycle parts, too; notice the bicycle tires in the back.

LADIES ON ONE SIDE, GENTS ON THE OTHER. On the left, we see shirtwaists on the counter and bolts of material behind it. On the right, we see men's hats and caps and collars on a rack—don't they look stiff! The boxes probably hold socks. From left to right, Blanche Silsby and Annie Houghton are behind the counter while Harley Cowles, Charles Hale, and Harry Silsby stand in the aisles of F.W. Silsby's dry goods and clothing store in the Eaton block, *c.* 1920.

JULIUS CAESAR EATON BUILT THIS UNIQUE BLOCK. It was built in 1893 with the tower-like structures adding a Victorian touch. J.C. sold stoves, hardware, and fashioned tinware on the premises. The *Lyndonville Journal* was printed upstairs, and F.W. Silsby & Co. showed off two fur coats outside their store, located on the right of the photograph. When Mr. Eaton had his store in Lyndon Corner, he sent peddler wagons out into the country with brooms and tinware. When he burned out at the Corner, he moved to Lyndonville and set up business in the Nichols Block, on the north side of Depot Street, until his own building (shown here) on the south side of Depot Street was finished. It was short-lived because it fell victim to the November 27, 1894 fire. He built another block with a plainer style, but it burned in 1924. By then Mr. Eaton retired instead of rebuilding.

PHOTOGRAPHER F.B. SNELLING. He framed these workmen who were building a new block for George Ide to replace the one he lost in the fire of 1894. The pile of bricks at left were no doubt salvaged from the Masonic Block. The stones in the foreground appear to be fill for the foundation of new buildings that replaced the burned blocks on the south side of the street.

THE CORNER GARAGE. Cars entered or departed from either Broad or Depot Streets. The Sunset Ballroom was upstairs, the bowling alley was in the basement, and originally, an automobile showroom was on the Depot Street side. There was an elevator that took cars to the second floor for storage. The corner was enclosed and is now occupied by the Western Auto store, facing Depot Street; the "lubritorium" is now Green Mountain Books and Prints on Broad Street.

BOUNTIFUL FRUIT IN 1911. A.F. Christopher appears to be really proud of his fruit display—bananas, Concord grapes, apples, and more. Though bananas grow pointing up, they were displayed hanging down. Grocers would take a large knife to cut off a "hand," or bunch, for a customer. With Mr. Christopher is E.J. Blodgett (right), a businessman from a nearby office.

NO GAS—SO WHAT! When gas was rationed during World War II, it was a real treat when Howard Little took Darling Inn guests and others for taxi rides around town.

W.F. Nicholson's Blacksmith Shop. It stood on Grove Street prior to and after the Vermont Tap & Die plant was built beside it. When American Saw & Tool Company of Louisville, Kentucky, bought the plant from C.H. Davis, the new owners enlarged the capacity of its operation by buying out the Diamond Bronze Company, a foundry, and Bill Nick's shop.

A Village Blacksmith. William Nicholson, the blacksmith, poses for this photo at his forge.

LYNDONVILLE UNITED METHODIST CHURCH. This image was taken in the early 1900s. The Methodists in Lyndonville met in a railroad shop, then in the village school or a store, until this church was built on Church Street around 1878. It has undergone many alterations and additions over the years.

THE ST. ELIZABETH CATHOLIC CHURCH. The church was built in 1892 of brick-Romanesque style after fire destroyed the wooden St. Martin Church. The steeple, the highest point in the village, was designed to hold the village clock. An agreement between the village trustees and Father Paquet in 1894 stated that Lyndonville would own and maintain the clock but the Catholic Society would manage it—one obligation being to wind it every week.

THE FIRST CONGREGATIONAL CHURCH OF LYNDONVILLE. Built in 1872, this church burned in 1967. A new church was constructed on the same foundation with the main door facing Park Street instead of Church Street as in the photograph. Lyndon Center's Main Street homes across the Passumpsic River (not visible), as well as its cemetery, can be seen in the background.

ST. PETER'S EPISCOPAL CHURCH OF LYNDONVILLE. This church was built in 1898 on an Elm Street lot bought from Elisha Bigelow for $1,000. The Gothic influence shows especially in the windows at each end of the church.

THE BANK. No, this building is not located in a frontier town, but is the temporary quarters in the well-established Lyndonville. Immediately after the disastrous fire in November 1894, the Lyndonville National Bank's treasurer, Luther B. Harris, gazed at the ruins of Ide Block where this bank, as well as the Lyndonville Savings Bank, burned. He assured burned-out real estate owners that money to rebuild would be provided. The next morning, while the ruins were still smoldering, the directors made it official.

THE NEW BANK. The directors instructed the officers of the bank to build a permanent fireproof building for its own use and to locate and design it "with a view to beautify and enrich the village." The new bank, erected on Broad Street, housed both the Lyndonville National and the Lyndonville Savings Banks. These two banks merged in 1922. This handsome building was replaced with a modern bank in 1960.

DECORATED FOR A SPECIAL OCCASION. Lyndonville Savings Bank and Trust Company treasurer, W.E. Riley, stands on the steps while workmen pose for the picture, *c.* 1922. We are intrigued with the reflection of the St. Elizabeth Catholic Church steeple in the window. The other window reflects trees but also seen is a bank employee behind the teller's wrought-iron grille. Since 1905, two Donatello lions have guarded the bank entrance. Treasurer Luther B. Harris, an amateur sculptor himself, was impressed with the Lion of the Republic in Florence, Italy. Through the famous American sculptor Larkin Mead, then visiting in Florence, he arranged for two lions to be cast in the original mold done centuries before by the Renaissance sculptor Donato di Nicola Bardi. The two lions were in keeping with the directors' desire to build a bank to beautify the village and show appreciation to the people for the confidence placed in them after the fire. Larkin Mead wrote to Mr. Harris, "They [the lions] will be great educators and will create a taste for the beautiful."

CAMP MEETING AT RAILROAD GROVE, 1900. The railroad company provided benches for three thousand people. It was a big outing for many. Besides driving themselves, many came from north and south of Lyndonville by train. Spiritual uplift may have been one reason a lot of people attended but it was also a social time. It was said there was a good deal of horse trading, swapping of jackknives, and other such activities, while the womenfolk exchanged patterns and recipes.

PARKING PLACES ALL FILLED. When the parking area was filled in the Grove, horses and buggies parked out on Main Street. They were sometimes lined all the way from the Grove to the fork in the road above the Lyndonville Creamery at the north end of Main Street.

NEW POST OFFICE IN LYNDONVILLE. This photograph illustrates the ground-breaking ceremony in 1959. Taking part were (left to right) village trustee Warner Scribner, owner and contractor Charles Petrie, selectman Dale Roundy, postmaster Robert F. Pierce, NVDA representative Carl "Joe" Gordon, postal clerk Lorin "Lonnie" Huntley, village trustee John Young, selectman Howard Johnson, selectman Howard Shonyo, Rotarian George Hopkins, and Robert Morreau. The old post office was in a block on Depot Street.

STORES OF LONG STANDING. The May Store was originally Scott McDowell's Variety Store. Later owners, the Morrissettes, named it the May Store, which has been continued (since 1972) by Alan and Denise Parent, who in time moved it to larger quarters on Memorial Drive. Joseph LeBlanc bought the Gray's Market and changed it to the English version of his own name, White Market; in the 1950s, he moved it into the former Plaza Theater nearby. The White Market was purchased by the Bona family in 1963. This photograph was taken c. 1948.

An Enterprising Young Lad. Conrad Spencer, eight years old in 1916, sold *Saturday Evening Post* and *Country Gentleman* magazines. He is on Depot Street, having picked up the latest issues at one of the drugstores. He earned a nickel for each magazine sold. When he had saved $5.00, a good neighbor, Mr. Griswold, took him to St. Johnsbury by train and he made a deposit in the Citizens Bank there. Before coming home they had an ice cream treat and then went to Moore and Johnson's store to visit.

Six
Made in Lyndon

BRINGING THE STORE TO THE COUNTRY. J.C. Eaton had a tinsmith shop and hardware store at Lyndon Corner. He sent peddler wagons into the country where people couldn't get into town often. Jim Webber, shown here at Damon's Crossing in Victory c. 1881, was instructed to sell brooms, tinware made by Eaton's shop, and other goods or trade for anything that could be turned into cash.

THE OLD WILDER MILL AND WATER RIGHTS. The mill was acquired by the Lyndonville Electric company in 1895–96. The mill wheels were torn out and dynamos installed with the capability of developing 640 horsepower. That was more than enough to light the 34 mercury vapor street lamps and incandescent lights in stores and residences. This was before the days of electric appliances and all else that is run by electricity.

A MODERN ELECTRIC PLANT. The new municipal electric plant was constructed in 1915. According to the *Vermont Union-Journal* of May 26, 1915, a large share of the credit for building up the prosperous, up-to-date village from the ruins of the old one destroyed by fire in 1894 was given to the enterprise of its citizens for installing the municipal electric and water plants.

YOUNG LADY WITH CAMERA. On June 26, 1916, she contemplates Little Falls at the Vail electric plant on the Passumpsic River.

THE VAIL PLANT. A hydro-electric facility was built by Theodore N. Vail at Little Falls, with direct lines to his Speedwell Farms and to his agricultural school at Lyndon Center. When the state of Vermont gave up the agricultural school in 1920, it went to Lyndon Institute. This included the Vail plant that the institute sold to the Lyndonville Electric Department in 1921. Lyndonville rebuilt it in 1949.

WETHERBEE, THE "TOP" TOP MANUFACTURERS. This woodworking and lumber dressing mill at Lyndon Corner survived the 1927 flood, whereas other Vermont mills were completely destroyed. Also, a big mill in Philadelphia burned down and, because Howard Wetherbee was known from his attendance at toy fairs, he filled orders meant for these flooded-out and burned mills. This made him the largest manufacturer of spinning tops in the world. The Wetherbee Mill, besides spinning tops, turned out chair spindles, baseball bats, candlepins, spools for ribbons, and more. Sometimes there were big piles of logs in the yard that customers brought in for Wetherbee to dress for lumber. This photograph was taken in 1915.

OSHA WOULDN'T APPROVE. Apparently in 1915, Ralph Davis had no problem standing ankle deep in shavings while operating a wood lathe at the Wetherbee Mill.

PAINTING THE TOPS AT WETHERBEE'S, 1915. Young ladies painted stripes on the spinning tops or toy tenpins by holding a small brush steady while the tops or tenpins revolved slowly on a spindle.

JOHN CHASE (1872–1960). Chase published a weekly paper formerly called the *Vermont Union*, which was originally started by his father, Charles M. Chase, in 1865. John took over when his father died in 1902. He bought the *Lyndonville Journal* three years later and changed the name of the paper to the *Vermont Union-Journal*. Bound editions and microfilm copies of these old newspapers at the Cobleigh Public Library have been a great resource for researchers of history. John was a staunch Democrat in a predominantly Republican town.

ELISABETH CHASE (1877–1948). She headed the Boys and Girls Home Project Clubs (forerunner of 4-H). Elisabeth started the Lyndon Maple Candy business to give work to young people needing money for school and hopefully to discourage the cutting of one of Vermont's great resources—the sugar maple orchards.

THE CHASE HOUSE AT LYNDON CORNER. This was the home of newspaper publisher John Chase and his wife, Elisabeth. It was here that Elisabeth made her famous Lyndon Maple Candies.

THE TEA ROOM AT THE CHASE HOUSE. As long as people were stopping to buy maple candies, Mrs. Chase began to offer homemade bread and butter. It soon followed that she not only had a tea room in her home and on the pleasant back porch, but, with ample room in the house, was offering room accommodations as well. This created even more opportunities for giving work to young people.

THE LYNDONVILLE CREAMERY AND CREW BEFORE 1913. The tall lady, center front, was Blanche Conner, office worker and manager. Her brother, Willis Conner, managed the creamery. Buttermaker Will Vancour and his wife lived upstairs. The creamery was completely destroyed by fire in 1913. The rebuilt plant included a separate office building. The Lyndonville Creamery Association was organized in 1890 by Washington Irving Powers, who was manager of Theodore N. Vail's Speedwell Farms and became the creamery's general manager and treasurer. It was the first separator creamery in this section of the state. Mr. Vail's dairy of more than a hundred thoroughbred cows was the leading contributor, but other dairies patronized the creamery as well. Butter churned here, made in prints of different sizes, was handsomely and appropriately stamped and packed in iced shipping trunks. "Butter that is churned here in the morning," reported the July 1, 1896 *Lyndonville Journal*, "is eaten at late dinner by the guests of the hotels and restaurants in Boston and New York." The railroad was the rapid transit of the day.

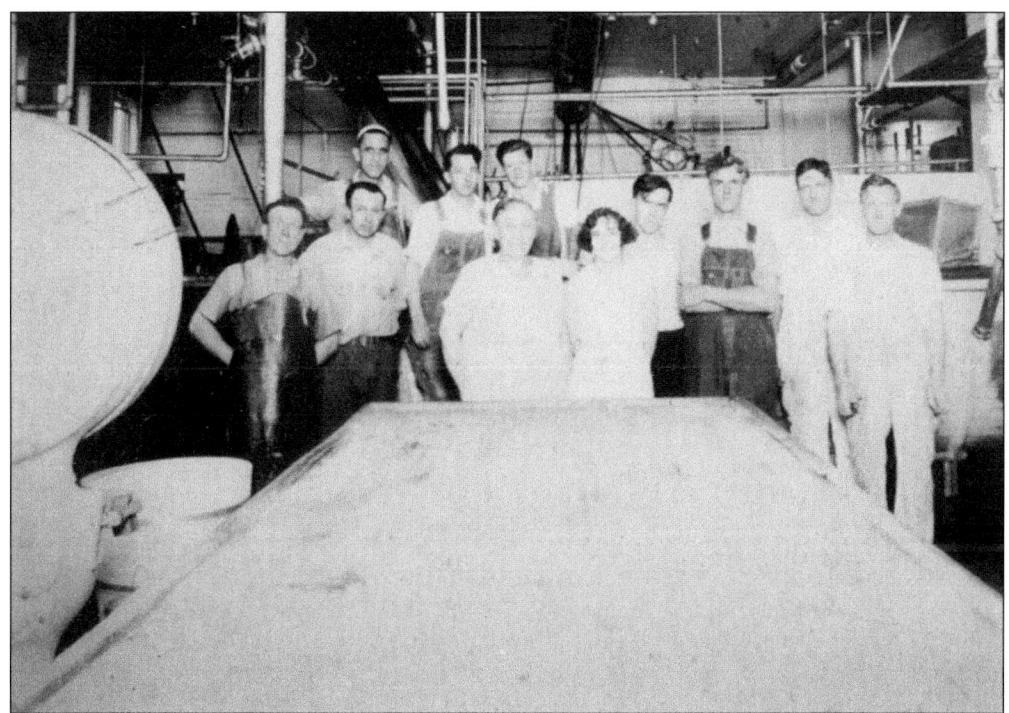

CHEESEMAKERS AT THE LYNDONVILLE CREAMERY. This photograph was taken c. 1935. Cottage cheese was made here as well as butter. Trucks transported these products to Boston every day, but local people could get cheese and butter at the creamery or in the stores.

KREAM OF THE KROP. This pretty lady holds a Kreamy Ice Kream sign in 1925. Signs like this were set up near stores that carried this popular ice cream made in Lyndonville by Wesley Emerson and Charles Stuart in a building behind the Stuart home on Center Street.

A LAZY DAY ON THE PASSUMPSIC. On July 7, 1916, this young lady seems to be enjoying a leisurely afternoon on the river at Lyndon Corner. Meanwhile in the building at the left, the home of Our Husbands Mfg. Co. of Veterinary Medicines, workers may be very busy turning out the product of the company.

THE MT. HUNGER STAVE MILL. The C.L. Wyman Lumbermill in 1895 on the road to East Burke used both steam and waterpower and employed 30 men. It was previously conducted by B.F. Lincoln, an associate of the Lyndon Halls Mill Company. The leading line here was spruce staves for the Horse Shoe Co., maker of kegs for horseshoe nails.

VERMONT TAP & DIE COMPANY. This company brought industry to Lyndonville at a time when the railroad strike of 1922 and the Depression had devastated the work opportunities here. This tool manufacturing company was originally in Newport. C.H. Davis bought out the stockholders and in 1930 moved the company to Lyndonville. Tap & Die is now a Division of Greenfield Industries. During World War II, it proudly flew the Army-Navy "E" (for Excellence) flag awarded on the recommendation of the War Production Board.

HEAT TREATMENT PROCESS. This operation at the Tap & Die was familiar to "Paddy" Davis, shown here in the early 1950s. This time-proven salt bath process is still used today.

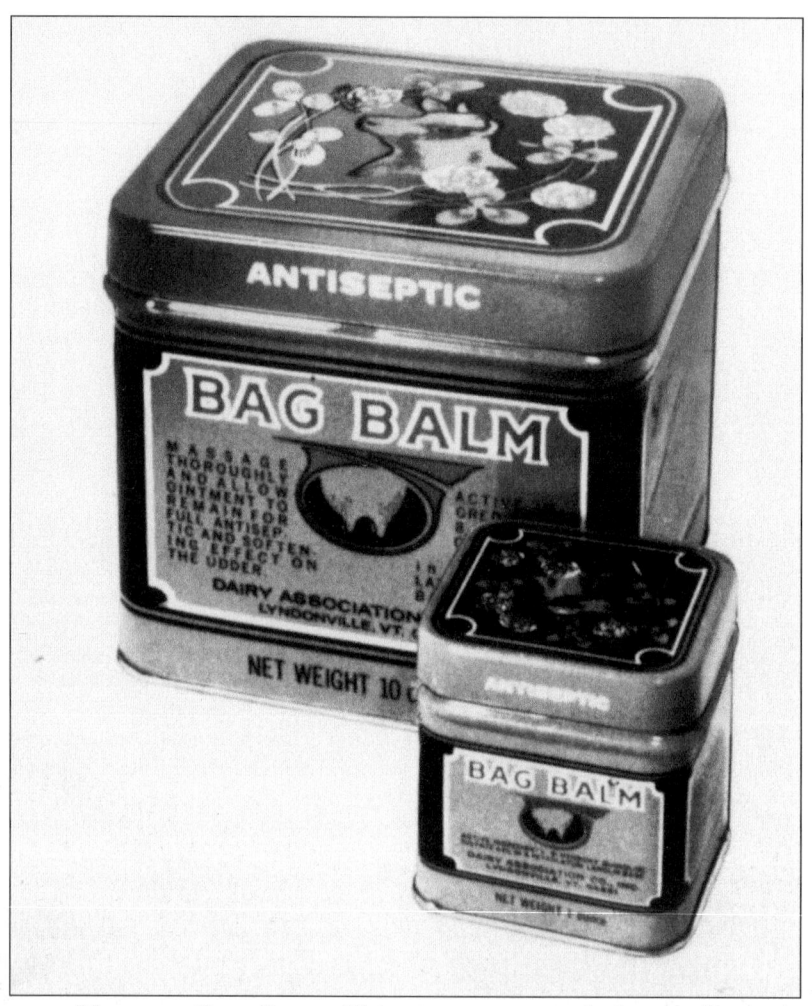

LYNDONVILLE, HOME OF BAG BALM. This ointment is made by the Dairy Association Company. Haddon Lyster started manufacturing Kow Kure in 1889, and John L. Norris Sr. bought the company around 1905 and started the manufacture of Bag Balm in 1908. This famous product, made right in the village of Lyndonville, is a healing agent for cows' udders. It is also a medicine cabinet staple, having been found excellent for human use as well—chapped hands, quilters' pricked fingers, scratches, skin cracks, and much more. In addition, people have found this versatile product handy for other purposes, squeaky bed springs or wheels, for example. The green cans with the pink Vermont clover are famous all over the world. The company makes other veterinary products, such as Tack Master for softening leather. The name Kow Kure was changed to Kow Kare in 1920 because of disallowance of the word implying cure. John L. Norris Jr. joined his father in 1934 after graduation from Lyndon Institute and has been with the company ever since.

Seven

Bad Times

THE WRECK OF '23. On the evening of July 24, 1923, a Canadian Pacific way freight met with a terrible accident north of Lyndonville near Webster Flats. A broken wheel cut off 200 feet of ties and some on the bridge. Thirteen of the train's 40 cars were wrecked, strewing automobiles, eggs, butter, produce, and lumber all over the field. As there were no passenger cars and the engine had crossed the bridge safely, no one was injured.

BUSINESS HARDLY MISSED A BEAT. The big fire of November 27, 1894, destroyed the Cheney Bros. drugstore and the W.D. Poole boot and shoe store among many others. Temporary quarters were raised for these two businesses on Church Street until new blocks were constructed.

DEPOT STREET RISES FROM THE ASHES. Lumber, scaffolding, and ladders for rebuilding after the 1894 fire show that a lively reconstruction era is underway. The photograph is before 1897 because the Dodge & Watson Block was built then, whereas the photograph shows the temporary building near front right, next to Silsby's Livery Stable. The building with the two-story porch is the rebuilt Webb's Hotel.

THE $500,000 FIRE. This catastrophe took half of Depot Street and seven lives in Lyndonville on January 21, 1924. Pictured here is the Hotel Lyndon (formerly Webb's) and the abandoned hose cart, now on display at the Shores Memorial Museum in Lyndon Center. The burned hotel was replaced by the Darling Inn.

SMOKY AND BLEAK. After the fire, half of Depot Street lay in ruins, not quite 30 years from the date of the devastating 1894 fire. The high brick wall was all that remained of the handsome Masonic Block. Reconstruction began right away, and more modern, less ornate buildings took shape along the street.

THE LYNDON STATION. This building probably did not have a basement to take the brunt of the force of the November 1927 floodwaters. The Chase Bridge stood but the road did not. This covered span was replaced by a concrete bridge in 1933. After the waters went down, people drove around as far as they could go to see the damage wrought by the destructive flooding.

LAKESIDE PROPERTY ON PARK AVENUE. The Passumpsic River flooded most of Lyndonville—except the side that headed uphill eastward. Harold Mason needed bread at his store in Lyndon Center, so he and two passengers rowed over to Lyndonville to restock. The loaves are in the white package visible in the boat. They are rowing past the Queen Anne style row of homes along Park Avenue.

THE BRIDGE STOOD, BUT THE TRACKS DID NOT. One aftermath of the great flood was the upheaval of railroad tracks and roads. This railroad bridge was near Red Village. Reconstruction began immediately and in his book, *Lights and Shadows of the 1927 Flood*, Charles T. Walter said, "It is not the Vermont way to whine or repine. Our feet are still on the ground and our faces are toward the sunrise."

THE CREAMERY BRIDGE. Butter tubs, milk cans, and other debris amassed at the covered bridge approaching the Lyndonville Creamery, seen at left, after the waters receded from the 1927 flood.

WORLD WAR II OBSERVATION POST. This post was on Skyline Drive on a hill above Lyndonville. The aircraft warning service volunteers carried identification cards showing photograph and signature. It was countersigned by the chief observer. The post was staffed 24 hours a day.

Description of Observer
(To be filled in by Chief Observer)

white	Medium
Race	Complexion
5'-6"	135
Height	Weight
brown	brown
Color Hair	Color Eyes

Leon E Hopkins
Signature of Chief Observer

This pass may be revoked at any time by the Chief Observer or any authorized representative of the First Interceptor Command.

AIRCRAFT WARNING SERVICE
U. S. ARMY
OBSERVER IDENTIFICATION

NAME   Emma D. Fletcher

STREET

CITY   Lyndonville   STATE, Vt.

The bearer is a civilian Volunteer in the U.S. Army Aircraft Warning Service. This pass must be used only in pursuance of his official duties.

HOLDER MUST SIGN HERE   301 3950

Emma D. Fletch

30B

IDENTIFICATION CARD. This is an example of the identification cards, front and back, carried by observers. The volunteers spent many hours at these posts. It was their duty to recognize and report any aircraft they spotted.

SAYING FAREWELL TO COMPANY D. In April 1917, at the Lyndonville railroad station, it appears that railroad workers and some band members were there to help send the troops off to war.

IT RAINED ON THEIR PARADE. Rain didn't stop these youngsters or all the others who observed the memory of departed soldiers on Memorial Day, 1950, as they paraded from Railroad Park in Lyndonville to the Lyndon Center Cemetery for appropriate ceremonies. Other groups such as the National Guard, Girl and Boy Scouts, war veterans, and many more joined in to pay their respects.

DENNIS DUHIGG OF LYNDON. He heeded President Lincoln's call, came home from Dartmouth College where he was a student, and almost single-handedly raised a company. This saved the town from a draft, and appreciative town fathers presented Dennis with this revolver and all the accouterments. He served in the 15th Regiment, Vermont Volunteers, and was killed at Winchester. His promotion to captain came posthumously.

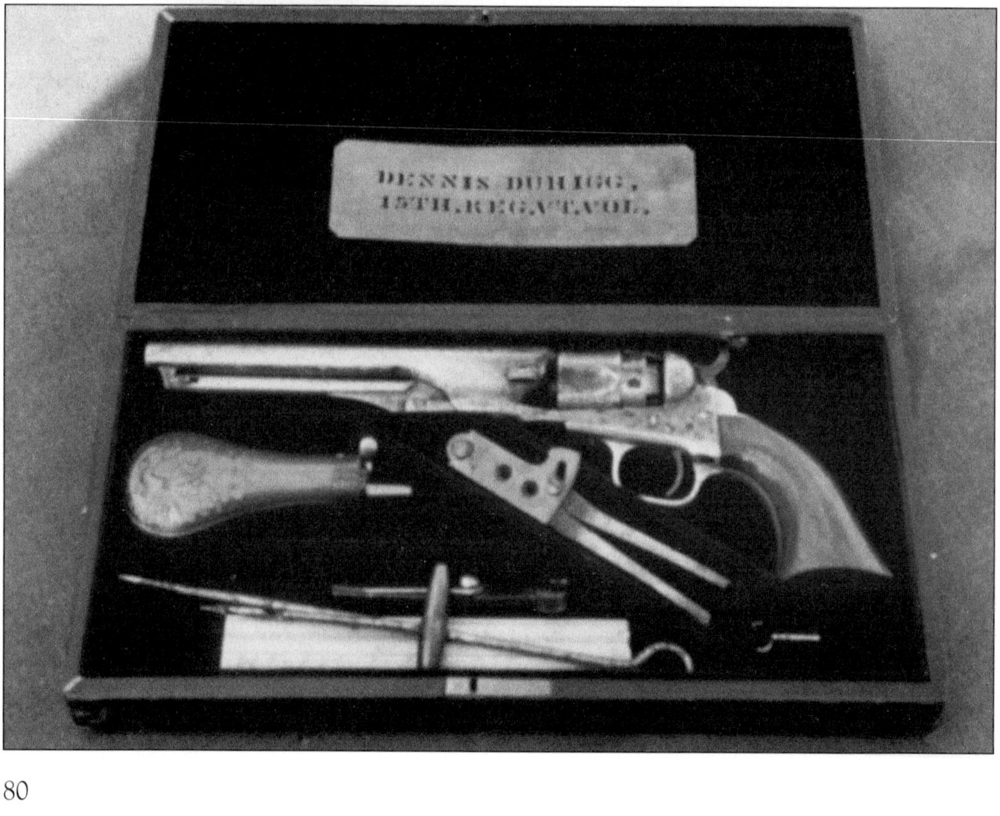

Eight
Good Times

CULTURE AND ENTERTAINMENT. In Lyndonville, entertainment could be found often in the Music Hall. The Village Improvement Society sponsored musicals from time to time with directors coming from Boston to put them on with all local talent. This photograph was taken *c.* 1900.

MUSIC HALL (VILLAGE HALL, OPERA HOUSE). On Broad Street (behind horse and wagon) right in the heart of Lyndonville stood the Music Hall, where silent movies, concerts, balls, plays, graduations, and other activities took place from the mid-1880s, when it was built, until people began to find entertainment away from home more and more. Built in 1884, it had a large hall and self-supporting balconies, so there were no posts needed underneath, leaving the whole floor unimpeded for all activities. Folding seats were attached in rows so that a whole row could be pushed under the back balcony. The basement held a kitchen, dining room, furnace room, water closets, and a lock-up used occasionally for someone who needed an overnight sobering up. It was the National Guard Armory for a few years and was eventually rented to a shoe factory in 1953 which burned down on October 23, 1954.

THE LYNDONVILLE MILITARY BAND. This photograph, taken *c.* 1898, depicts the bandstand on Depot Park (seen in the photograph on page 82). References to bands in Lyndonville go back as far as 1867 under different names, such as Lyndonville Brass Band, Lyndonville Cornet Band, and eventually Lyndonville Military Band. Because the band accompanied the Grand Army of the Republic to national encampments so often, it became the official state band for several later encampments. When it went to Salt Lake City in 1909, it was the first band to play in the Mormon Tabernacle. The bandstand was moved from the railroad depot site to the common on Main Street, now called Bandstand Park. Sometimes they played concerts in the Music Hall. For more than 100 years, weekly outdoor band concerts in the park have been a summertime tradition.

LYNDONVILLE BAND AT CALEDONIA COUNTY FAIR, 1939. Before the band got their new uniforms, they looked smart in white pants, shirts, and black bow ties. Their snappy new uniforms, green with gold braid, arrived in 1941.

THE LYNDONVILLE MILITARY BAND. This photograph was taken in 1946 on the steps of the Cobleigh Public Library. Their practice room was in the library basement. Perley Harris, director for many years, is at left. Gerald Aubin, almost hidden at right, and Russell Wilson, with drum at right, are still playing with the band.

FLAGS ADORN WEBB'S HOTEL. The carriage is full of young ladies ready to help celebrate a patriotic occasion. In the early days of the village, Charles Webb converted a building on Depot Street into this hotel, opening it in 1877, the heyday of the railroad. It burned down in 1894, was rebuilt, and then burned down again in 1924. After the 1894 fire, the replacement building, designed by architect Lambert Packard, opened on June 8, 1895, the first new building in Lyndonville to be completed after the blaze. It was described in the *Vermont Union* as follows: "Size 42 by 50, three stories, a convenient basement with a large boiler room, billiard room, barber saloon [*sic*], laundry room, two card rooms, and a room for the bootblack." The first floor contained a writing and reading room, a ladies parlor, toilet room, water closet, dining room to seat 100 guests, good kitchen, and store room. There were 40 sleeping rooms on the two floors above. The hotel was heated by steam and had call bells in all parts. For many years the hotel, which later owners renamed Hotel Lyndon, was a vital part of the village.

TIGER 1, LYNDONVILLE'S FIRST VOLUNTEER FIRE COMPANY. Looking sharp in their uniforms, the volunteer fire company poses on Railroad Park (also known as Depot Park) for the big Lyndon Centennial parade on July 4, 1891. Fires generally were fought in the early days with quickly formed bucket brigades, but in 1883, Lyndonville trustees Fletcher and Eastman purchased a Hannaman hand fire engine in Franklin, New Hampshire, with 150 feet of hose, a hose carrier, nozzles, and according to the *Vermont Union*, "everything that goes with the machine." The Tiger Company raised money for striking uniforms—dark blue pants, white flannel shirt with blue shield on the chest, and white buttons lettered with the words, Tiger 1. In addition, they wore a black leather belt with white trimmings and a straight-visor, dark blue cap, with a brass badge embossed with a steam fire engine on the front. They must have looked smart in the centennial parade. Behind them is a float with flags and girls in costume. The other float held 44 girls, each with state banners representing the 44 states at that time. Behind them are Williams Street, the St. Martin Catholic Church, and the freight station.

BOOSTING "ME AND OTIS" AT THE MUSIC HALL TONIGHT. This show was performed by Lyndon Institute students in 1911. Before radio, this was a popular way to advertise shows and entertainment—drive around town and let people know about it. Boosters sometimes used megaphones to get the message across. Would the bucket and fish basket indicate at least one fishing scene in the show?

REDPATH CHAUTAUQUA. This show brought a week of culture and entertainment to Lyndonville almost every year from 1915 until 1933. It was a welcome sight when the big tent set up on the Darling meadow. A drawing from this photograph is the logo for flyers announcing a one-day Chautauqua, a kind of renewal event held each year since the Lyndon Bicentennial in 1991. This photograph was taken August 29, 1916.

CELEBRATING THE HARD ROAD. Motorcycle cop Harry Dickens leads the parade between Wells River and Lyndonville (now Route 5) on May 1, 1931, as it comes along Broad Street toward Depot Street. The road from Wells River to Derby was known as Indian Joe Trail. Vermonters did not want to go into debt to build roads to "get Vermont out of the mud," but the flood of 1927 may have accelerated the work.

VIP'S AT THE CEREMONIES IN LYNDONVILLE. All gathered to celebrate the new cement road—C.H. Davis (left), owner of Vermont Tap & Die; Governor Stanley Wilson (second from left); Roland Sundown as "Indian Joe" (fourth from left); State Highway Board member, Lyndon's own W. Arthur Simpson (seventh from left with open overcoat). Other state officials and highway department engineers also posed with these men for the photograph.

AN EXCITING TIME. Talkies came to town with the building of the Gem Theater on Elm Street. The opening movie was *The Grand Parade*. All the businesses in the village joined in the celebration at the dedication, May 31, 1930, running ads in the papers, offering special discounts, and making it a very eventful day.

THE REDMEN. The Great Council of the United States Improved Order of Red Men were 13 tribes to match the 13 colonies. They were photographed gathering here in a celebration at the fairgrounds. This fraternal society was impressed with the equality of the Native Americans because all could vote in Council meetings. The order adopted the motto, "Freedom, Friendship, and Charity," qualities they admired in the Native American tribes. The St. Johnsbury Order that included men from Lyndon disbanded in the early 1930s.

For a Pleasant Auto Ride and Good Things to eat Motor to

Y^e Olde Brick Tea Shoppe

LYNDON CORNER, VT.
On State Road
Seven miles north of St. Johnsbury.

Tea	5c	Milk	5c
Coffee	10c	Lemonade	5c
Chocolate	10c	Choice Sodas	5c

Sandwiches 5 and 10c.   Club Sandwiches
Lyndon Nut Bread, by loaf, 30c.   Cake by loaf.
Salads
Griddle Cakes with Pure Maple Syrup
Omelets 15c
Meals served at all hours.
Fresh Maple Candies   Fresh Salted Nuts   Cakes
Ice Cream

YE OLDE BRICK TEA SHOPPE. This shop at Lyndon Corner speaks for itself in the menu shown here.

A PLEASANT SUMMER AFTERNOON. Besides tea and food, some needlework items were offered for sale inside Ye Olde Brick Tea Shoppe. The Lyndon Carriage Company's carriage shop burned down and owner S.S. Mattocks sold the blacksmith shop and grounds to the Lyndon Improvement Society. It was a perfect place to stop after a pleasant auto ride for good things to eat.

Nine

Sports and Recreation

ALL EYES ON THE SKI JUMPER. A skier takes off from the Lyndon Outing Club's (LOC) 35-meter jump. Many high school and college Nordic, Alpine, and jumping meets were held here, some New England and some national. Numerous LOC skiers went on to compete in other parts of the country. The LOC is a still-thriving volunteer, community- and family-oriented club, organized in 1937.

WHEN LYNDON OUTING CLUB WENT TO THE DOGS. In the 1940s and 1950s, New England Championship dog sled races were an exciting part of the LOC Carnival during the week of Washington's Birthday. Depot Street, in downtown Lyndonville, was the starting point where a crowd gathered by the Darling Inn to watch the dogs take off. For a number of years a queen was crowned at the Carnival Ball in the Sunset Ballroom. LOC began in the Baril pasture on Hog Street (now Lily Pond Road) with a lighted hill, a 250-foot rope tow, and a small warming cabin. In 1947, LOC moved its equipment and the cabin to the Shonyo Hill, the present location. The cabin has been enlarged, a 1,500-foot T-Bar installed (1961), and more trails have been developed. The Dub Hill rope tow is exclusively for beginners (children or adults), until they are ready for the T-Bar. The Outing Club has always had night skiing, quite a change from the days when eager skiers ran down their car batteries shining lights on a hill so they could ski after working hours. The 1950 carnival featured an Honest Abe snow sculpture in Bandstand Park (below).

HERE THEY COME DOWN THE ELM-LINED MAIN STREET SPEEDWAY! (1948) Main Street was noted for two things—its beautiful elm trees arching over the street and the winter horse races. Impromptu races about the turn of the century, usually a driver of a sleigh or delivery cart challenging another, prompted a group of horsemen to form the Lyndonville Driving Club in 1907, "for clean sport conducted in a gentlemanly manner." It was a major winter pastime for many years and received widespread notice from the media, including *Life Magazine* and Boston papers. When the horsemen approached the village trustees in December 1907 to request approval for Saturday races, one trustee said, "I'd like to see that myself." A quarter-mile speedway was measured off, and trustee Austin Houghton scraped the street with railroad carsills. Stores closed from 2:00 to 4:00 p.m. on race day, Depot Street was roped off, the corners policed, the crowds gathered, and the race was on—with sleighs, no less. Later on, the horsemen found racing sulkies more to their liking.

THE DRIVING CLUB BANQUET, 1908. The final Driving Club event each winter was the Washington's Birthday race with a banquet in the evening where the winners received their ribbons and silver cups; no money was involved in these races (at least not officially). The first one was an oyster stew supper with sugar-on-snow in the GAR Hall. After that, the banquets were held in one of the several hotels.

CROWDS GATHERED TO WATCH THE RACES. As we see in this view, the crowds filled the streets. Some probably brought their sulkies on the sleds shown in this early racing photograph.

A SLEIGH RIDE. This activity was the height of enjoyment in winter. The young lad, Paul Fisher in the Mt. Hunger district, liked to hitch up his horse, Peanut, and take advantage of the fresh snow.

THE SWIMMING POND AT VAIL'S MANSION. In the 1930s and 1940s, young people headed for the swimming holes in the Passumpsic River. Sometimes they took advantage of the pond at Vail's Mansion for summer fun. One former Lyndon Center resident recalled that it was an annual contest to see who would be the first to "get wet all over" in the spring. The winner was awarded the title of "The Bravest of the Brave."

FISHER FIELD. In 1968, the Fisher family on Fletcher farm leased their former 4-acre hayfield to the Lyndonville Boys Baseball (now Lyndonville Youth Baseball because Little League and Babe Ruth baseball are open to girls). For years a nine-hole golf course and a skeet shooting range were in the nearby Fletcher pasture. This seems to have become a recreational area, as the former Shonyo farm hill across from the ball field is the site of the Lyndon Outing Club.

LYNDONVILLE BOYS BASEBALL. The league was named before girls began to play. Here we have Yankees, Red Sox, Giants, Dodgers, and Braves making up the teams that played each other. This was at Victory Field near Powers Park, but it was low-lying land near the river and often remained wet rather late in the spring—that was the reason the group looked for a new playing field.

SWIMMING TEAM AT POWERS PARK (1973). Under the auspices of the Lyndonville Village Improvement Society (VIS), the eight-week summer program keeps children, ages up to 18, busy with swimming and tennis lessons and crafts, as well as a reading program in conjunction with the Cobleigh Public Library. Washington Irving Powers acquired the old Railroad Grove from the Boston & Maine Railroad in 1915 and bequeathed it to the VIS for a community park.

THE FENTON CHESTER ARENA. It opened in 1964 and is managed by the Lyndon Area Sports Association. The arena is the home of the Lyndon Area Youth Hockey and the Lyndon Institute Vikings hockey teams. Figure skating is taught here, and an excellent ice show is staged annually by skaters from the ages of four through adult. Time is also scheduled for recreational skating.

HORSE PULLING. This sport has long been a feature of the Caledonia County Fair in Lyndon. Today a new and improved larger pulling ring has been built and the bank terraced for better seating and viewing. The first event held on this site was a Fourth of July celebration in 1877 when the Lyndon Park Association leased 20 acres (the present fairgrounds), erected a grandstand, and set out a one-half–mile racing track. Fourth of July celebrations and fairs with exhibits, entertainment, fireworks, and trotting races were annual events until 1902, when they were given up and the site reverted to farmland. In 1932, horsemen started jogging their horses at the old track and decided to organize the Community Fair Association. St. Johnsbury had given up the county fair held there since 1846. The Community Fair discontinued around 1938 and reorganized as the Caledonia County Fair. In 1955, the grounds were officially designated Mountain View Park to honor the memory of longtime fair president, Lyndonville businessman, and enthusiastic horseman, Charles Willoughby, who often referred to it by that name.

Ten
Getting Around

THE "AIRLINE." This photograph, taken on March 23, 1917, depicts the passenger train as it has just passed Folsom's Crossing and is approaching Lyndonville.

PASSENGER STATION. "Best on the line," said the *Vermont Union* in regard to this station when it was built in 1867. The building was torn down by the Canadian Pacific Railway in 1974. This photograph was taken *c.* 1909.

A PROUD GROUP OF RAILROAD SHOP WORKERS. As diesel engines began to replace steam locomotives by the mid-twentieth century, the railroad shops became more and more unnecessary and finally closed altogether.

100

CANADIAN PACIFIC RAILWAY ENGINE NO. 6142. As the engine stands ready (steam is seen puffing out from a valve near the front), conductor Clayton Libbey, brakeman James Austin, fireman Pliny "Jake" Burns, and engineer Travis "Ted" Blaisdell pose (from left to right) for a photograph.

FREIGHT WAS BIG BUSINESS IN LYNDONVILLE. Looking up from their paperwork are, from left to right, as follows: (front row) Wallace Roberts and unidentified; (back row) Alphonse Aubin, Edwin Daniels, and Herbert Hubbard. The photographs of President William H. Taft, right, and Vice-President James S. Sherman would indicate a date between 1909 and 1912.

WHAT THE WELL-DRESSED BICYCLIST WORE. The bicycle craze hit town in the 1880s and became fun, recreation, and eventually a mode of transportation to and from work until people whizzed along in a merry Oldsmobile. Lucius Park dressed in his best cycling outfit, including fancy-topped knee hose, for this studio photograph by F.B. Snelling of Lyndonville in 1890.

WHOSE PARKING PLACE IS THIS? There seems to be a lot going on in Lyndonville. David Silsby's Livery Stable, partly visible on the right, was torn down in 1905 to make room for the Cobleigh Public Library. The temporary building set up after the November 1894 fire, until the Dodge & Watson Block was built on that site, dates this photograph 1895 or 1896.

ON THE WAY CAMPING. That title was given to this image by the photographer on August 2, 1916. These campers seem to be well equipped as they start out from Hadleyville.

A JOLLY GOOD TIME WAS HAD BY ALL. Lyndonville Creamery workers were photographed while on an outing in the early 1900s. They may have been going on a train excursion, as they are stopped by the station (not shown in the photograph). The hotel behind the train is the Union House, later known as the Pleasant View House.

FILLING STATION. Stations like Allen Hunter's sprang up all over the country when automobiles really began to replace horses. Anti-knock gasoline was 19¢ per gallon (including 5¢ tax) in 1935 when Clyde Hunter took this photograph. Phillip Morris cigarettes were available inside as well as candy, gum, and small automotive needs. The barn behind the station was made over into a residence.

DRIVE IN TODAY. This is a thoughtful postcard reminder from the Corner Garage in 1940. On the reverse it says, "Your car was lubricated at 16,044 miles. You've got enough to think about without trying to remember when your car needs its next Mobilubrication and inspection." Bernard Mitchell (left) and Kenneth Wheeler are ready to lube while a mobile service trainer encourages them.

RFD Route No. 1, U.S. Mail. The "swift completion of his rounds" probably depended on how fast a horse the carrier was driving.

Through Rain, Sleet, and Probably Mud. These RFD carriers, *c.* 1912, were ready to deliver mail to the patrons on the three rural routes. Clarence Batchelder, Harris Allen, and Lucius Park (from left to right) loaded the mail from the back door of the Lyndonville post office on Church Street. The front door opened on Depot Street.

HAVE GROCERIES, WILL TRAVEL. In the early 1930s, Glenn Johnson and family, of Lyndon Corner, were in the Traveling Grocery business, taking the store to outlying farms, logging camps, and other remote settlements. Every morning these grocers donned white suits freshly washed and ironed by Mrs. Johnson. World War II, with its rationing of many goods, gasoline, and tires, ended this enterprise. Eddie Walsh (left) and Homer Johnson stand by one of the trucks in 1925.

GRADING MAIN STREET. This photograph was taken *c.* 1920 probably in early spring, as the elm trees are just budding. Ed Meyette's team on the lead and Eldon Hovey on back are operating the grader along Main Street. People sometimes hired out themselves and their teams to the town or village when they were not haying or logging.

LAYING THE DUST. It took a three-horse hitch, handled by Lyndonville trustee Austin Houghton, to pull this water wagon seen here on Main Street. The bunting and flags draping the buildings would indicate that the town may have been in preparation for a Fourth of July celebration *c.* 1908.

DR. A.A. CHENEY WITH HIS NEW HUDSON. This was probably easier than harnessing up a horse to make house calls out in the country—after he got used to it. It is said that when he first drove into the garage, he tried to stop the machine by hollering "Whoa!," but it didn't stop and demolished a sleigh at the back of the garage.

Up, Up, and Away! After the hay was stored in the barn, the Merriam hayfield served as a landing strip before local airports were built. Luella Merriam stands by the two men, identified as an airplane parachute jumper and a mechanic. Luella ventured to take one ride in 1931. With a river on one side and trees on the other side of the field, the pilot had to be pretty accurate.

Eleven
Education:
Kindergarten through College

CARL SIMPSON. This boy may have brought an apple to the teacher, Pearl Moore, when he attended the Squabble Hollow one-room school years ago, but during the school's centennial celebration in 1981, he gave her a big smack on the cheek. The school is now a private residence.

St. Martin's Catholic School. In the late nineteenth century, French Canadians came to Lyndonville to work on the railroad sections. Many could not speak English, and the school was opened for young children in 1881. It closed in 1893, and the children then attended the public schools. The Catholic schoolhouse became a private residence.

Vail Hill School. This schoolhouse is an example of an older-day one-room school, probably early 1900s. Pupils at this school were mostly children of Speedwell Farms employees.

RED VILLAGE SCHOOL. This and Squabble Hollow School were the last two of Lyndon's one-room schools to close (in 1991). The original building goes back many years but was replaced in 1899 by a new schoolhouse, the one shown here in 1978.

LYNDON CENTER SCHOOL (1865–1900). After a new school was built, this one (far right) housed cemetery equipment, hence the double-door cut in the center. The building left of the school was the hearse house and at far left the horse shed. The old Universalist chapel, turned into a horse training stable, stood on the other side of the schoolhouse, and some people deplored that the children played between the tomb and the manure pile.

INTRIGUING PHOTOGRAPH. These children posed in front of the Lyndon Center School in 1898. It is obvious that it was the era of the cape, or coats, and jackets with capes (or capelets). The Sears & Roebuck catalog for that year shows these same styles. Notice that the school had two entrances, one for boys and one for girls.

THE WOODEN GRADED SCHOOL. The school was built in 1868 at the end of School Street (now Maple Street) when the new village was growing rapidly because of the railroad. It had two rooms, which were ample for the time being. When the new brick graded school was constructed in 1905, the old structure was bought by Theodore Harris and moved to become part of his home at Lyndon Center.

LYNDONVILLE GRADED SCHOOL. A handsome brick building, with bulls-eye glass front doors, replaced the old wooden graded school—once called West Street, then Maple Street, now Park Avenue. Eventually the archway was hidden by a covered entry that was believed necessary for safety's sake.

MARTIN E. DANIELS, SCHOOL SUPERINTENDENT (1908–1941). Daniels is pictured here in his office at home on South Street. There were as many as 35 miles between some of the 52 schools in the North Central Union, and there were times when he had to walk some of those miles. He visited all the schools regularly to check on needs and problems. In his 1915 annual report to the Lyndonville school directors, he deplored the use of tobacco by some of the pupils.

THE FIRST ACADEMY IN LYNDON. Chartered in 1831, this academy sometimes held as many as one hundred students. Closing in 1866 or 1867, it was auctioned off and became a private residence. For a short time it was Woodlawn Hotel and then a private residence again. The belfry and bell were transferred to the new Academy and Graded School built nearby.

LYNDON ACADEMY AND GRADED SCHOOL. Built in 1872, this school was the Lyndon Corner Graded School until 1991. It was an academy for only a short period because more and more high school students attended Lyndon Institute at Lyndon Center. It was topped by the belfry and bell from the old academy. The handsome arched doorway was hidden when it seemed necessary in modern times to build a protective structure over the steps.

THOMPSON HALL. Pictured here is the entire student body during the 1911–12 academic year. The Lyndon Literary and Biblical Institution was chartered in 1867 by Baptist leaders and local businessmen. Named for Sumner Thompson, an early benefactor of the institution, the building burned in January 1922. Students finished the school year in various places and were in the new building by December of that same year.

AS YOU LIKE IT. The Lyndon Institute Class of 1905 went all out with their version of this Shakespeare play. They are, from left to right, as follows: (sitting) Earl Davis, Herbert Burnham, Albert Riley, and Grace Deos; (standing) Glenn Buck, Edith Gray, Ed Carpenter, Fred Rainey, Ida Flower, May Campbell, Faye Newell, Grace Finney, Arthur Simpson, Dana Smith, Walter Cleary, Flossie Chesley, Frank McGinnis, and Carl Smith.

THE NEW INSTITUTE BUILDING. The building stands proudly on the rise overlooking the campus and athletic field on the same spot where Thompson Hall once stood. The school's name, long known informally as Lyndon Institute, was confirmed legally in 1923. Since this photograph was taken *c.* 1925, a gymnasium and auditorium wing has been added, to the left, and a cafeteria wing with classrooms above, to the right. The institute, a private school, serves as the designated high school for Lyndon and surrounding towns.

LYNDON INSTITUTE OBSERVES ITS CENTENNIAL. The celebration took place in 1967 with festivities and a big parade. The many floats were designed by art teacher Bertha Koury and constructed by eager students, parents, and townspeople. This one represents Baptist clergy and area businessmen who chartered the institution in 1867. By the time the school was built and got underway, the first class to graduate was in 1873—just one student. In 1997, the graduating class numbered 129.

THEODORE NEWTON VAIL (1845–1920). The founder and first president of the American Telephone and Telegraph Company, Vail was a benefactor of Lyndon Institute, moving buildings around to form the quadrangle that comprises the institute's beautiful campus. In 1912, he hired educator Ozias D. Mathewson to be principal, a post he held for 30 years.

THE AGRICULTURAL SCHOOL DAIRY BARN. This barn was built by the "Aggie" boys on the Lyndon Institute grounds in 1913, as well as the creamery seen at the left. The barn and creamery currently serve other vocational purposes.

THE GIRLS ARE BUSY, TOO. T.N. Vail did not forget the young women in his school. He made sure there were domestic science classes at Lyndon Institute. This is the home economics cooking class, 1913–14, at Thompson Hall, Lyndon Institute's original school building which burned in 1922.

LYNDON STATE COLLEGE. Theodore N. Vail turned a simple farmhouse into a palatial mansion on this beautiful hilltop because he loved the vista. Although Vail never foresaw that his home would become the site of Lyndon State College, he was a great believer in education and his personal vision went far beyond the present.

LYNDON INSTITUTE GRADUATE, 1910. Dr. Venila Lovina Shores, Lyndon Center, earned her Ph.D. degree in history from Johns Hopkins University. For over 20 years she gathered, researched, and meticulously documented Lyndon history each summer while at home from her duties as head of the history department at Florida State College for Women. When Dr. Shores retired in 1957, a friend speaking of her Tallahassee years said, "Venila is an independent soul, with a decent respect for the opinions of others, with courage to speak her own mind. She speaks plainly, honestly—there is no guile nor flattery in her, but a sense of humor makes her sometimes salty company." She also said, "Venila is a handy woman with tools—hammer, hoe, pruning shears, egg beater, needle, pipe wrench, and typewriter." Another friend said, "Few people approach life with [such a] serenely unhurried attitude." To those who knew her, these words summed up the life of Dr. Venila Shores. She died in 1980, deeding her family home and its contents to the Town to serve as the museum for the Lyndon Historical Society.

Twelve

Recycling:
New Uses for Old

RAILROAD SHOPS BUILT IN 1866–67. These shops employed a goodly number of people. Now the railroad is no longer based in Lyndonville since the last owner, Canadian Pacific Railway, took the operation to Canada. This shop later housed a woodworking and fence business. Now one of the shops is headquarters for the Northeast Kingdom Waste Management District and a matching one is used for the recycling center. All other buildings were torn down by the railroad company.

FROM SCHOOL TO MUNICIPAL OFFICES. The Lyndonville Graded School, once filled with children, lessons, textbooks, chalk, and all that goes with grade schools, has become the Municipal Office Building without change to its original exterior. It houses town and village offices, as well as the Caledonia North Supervisory Union. A handsome traditional style brick school was built in 1991 on Lily Pond Road, serving all the schoolchildren in Lyndon village and town.

FROM SCHOOL TO MEDICAL CENTER. The Lyndon Corner Graded School closed in 1991, and the pupils in this school, too, joined all the rest of the town's students in the new Town School. Dr. Lloyd Thompson and Dr. John Elliott bought the Corner School and changed it into a medical center now affiliated with the Dartmouth-Hitchcock Clinic. The exterior faithfully retains the original appearance.

FROM PENCILS TO COMPUTERS. Built in 1900, this school at Lyndon Center also closed its doors in 1991. It was known as the Campus School because it was once a practice facility for the teachers training at the Lyndon Normal School affiliated with the institute. Lyndon Institute acquired and renovated the building; the institute kept the last remodeled graded school appearance and made it the business education department with all the necessary computer systems for training in modern business methods.

A GEM IN THE GREEN, C. 1940. This inn opened in 1930, taking the place of the former Webb's (later Hotel Lyndon) that burned in 1924, and it was named Darling Inn for Elmer Darling, a generous subscriber. In 1964, Mr. and Mrs. Andrew Janis acquired the inn and operated it as a convalescent home. The Northern Community Investment Corporation made extensive renovations and changed it to the Darling Inn Apartments for senior citizens in 1980. The term, "Gem in the Green," has been adopted informally as a sobriquet for the whole town of Lyndon.

A HANDSOME COUNTRY HOME WITH A CUPOLA. This home was built in 1867 by Benjamin Franklin Lincoln, a Lyndon Mill owner, and later became the home of A.N. Wetherbee. It has been a nursing home since the 1950s, now the Pines, a rehabilitation and health center. Residents enjoy watching the children across the road coming and going to the Riverside School. Sometimes the children stop in to visit.

RIVERSIDE, A STATELY HOME IN HAPPYTOWN. This was an area where people held neighborhood gatherings at the drop of a hat. It was built in 1866 by Dudley Pettingill Hall, a prominent Lyndon lumberman. In 1981, Riverside changed from a residence to a private school for grades four through eight, where Latin and Greek are included in the curriculum.

N.A. McDonald, Blacksmith & Horse Shoer. That was long ago, until the early 1900s. Later on it was the shop of blacksmith and horse shoer John Stafford. This building has gone through several recycling processes, such as a paint shop, storage shed, and other usage. Today it is the Carpet Connection, a thriving business at the east end of Depot Street.

The Christian Science Church (1956–1976). This church was located on Center Street, Lyndonville. After the church closed, it was a private residence until 1983. Then Lyndonville Office Equipment acquired the property and moved from smaller quarters on Main Street. This photograph was taken c. 1970.

UNIVERSALIST CHAPEL. This chapel, at Lyndon Center, *c.* 1890, was built in 1849 near the town cemetery. A golden decoration on the roof, the Angel Gabriel blowing his horn, was stolen in 1883 and never recovered. By the late 1880s, the building had fallen into disrepair and was sold. According to the *Vermont Union* in November 1895, a syndicate of horse-flesh enthusiasts bought it and turned it into a horse training and livery stable. The old church-turned-stable burned down in 1938.

NEW UNIVERSALIST CHURCH. This building was constructed in Lyndonville *c.* 1900. When membership dropped and the church could not support itself, the Universalist Society deeded it to the Village Improvement Society in 1944 and named it the Bemis Community House in honor of church benefactor Joshua Bemis. In 1977, employees of the Vermont Tap & Die purchased it and renamed it the Tom Breslin Community Center.

THE METHODIST CHURCH AT LYNDON CORNER. This church, built in 1839, served the Methodists for a long time. As people became more mobile and attendance fell off, it was sold and the new owner set up a secondhand store there. In the path of the throughway, Interstate 91, it was torn down along with a number of houses on both sides of the street, including these seen in the photograph.

THE PUDDING HILL SCHOOL. The schoolhouse was moved not a far distance from its original location to become part of the Caledonia County State Airport. Here it is used for meetings and training classes, including the Junior Civil Air Patrol. Most other one-room schools became residences. This photograph is dated 1978.

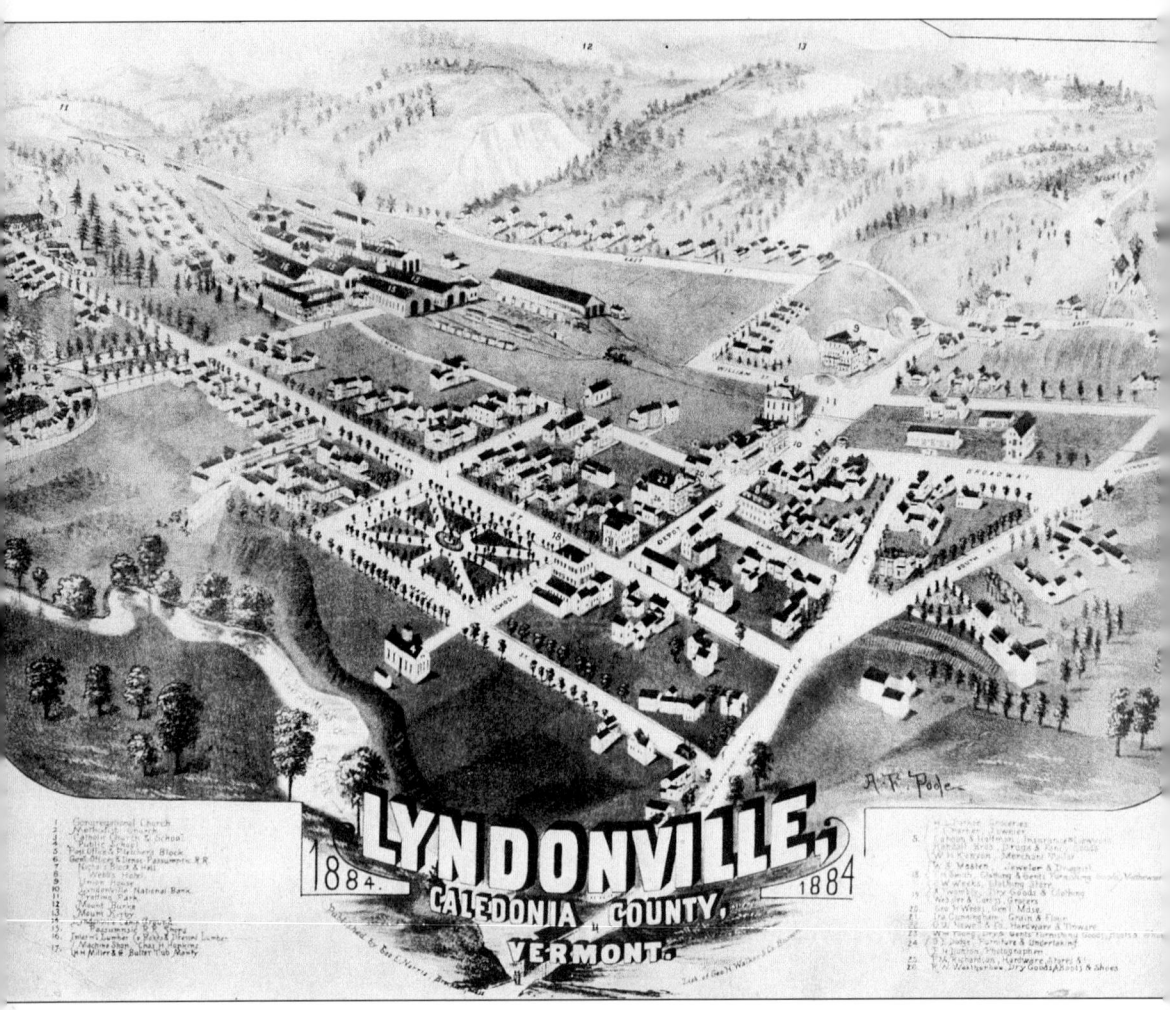

LYNDONVILLE,
CALEDONIA COUNTY,
VERMONT.
1884.   1884.